W9-BMC-252

THE KISS
Love Stories from North America

There are many different kinds of love story. There are simple love stories, where a boy meets a girl, they fall in love, get married, and everything ends happily. There are stories where everything does not end happily, and stories where the path of true love is full of problems and arguments, mistakes and misunderstandings.

In *The Bride Comes to Yellow Sky*, Jack and his new wife are returning to Jack's home in Yellow Sky, Texas, and they find a most surprising – and dangerous – welcome waiting for them. In *A Seashore Wooing* a girl meets a boy, but they have a great problem – and the name of the problem is Aunt Martha. *A White Heron* is a very different kind of love story. A little girl discovers in herself a love for the natural world – a love that is stronger than the need for money or the wish to please a new friend. And in *By Courier* a young lady refuses to speak to her young man. But why? What has he done wrong?

But the volume begins with the story called *The Kiss*. Be careful who you kiss, and when you do it!

OXFORD BOOKWORMS LIBRARY
Human Interest

The Kiss
Love Stories from North America

Stage 3 (1000 headwords)

PAPL
DISCARDED

Series Editor: Jennifer Bassett
Founder Editor: Tricia Hedge
Activities Editors: Jennifer Bassett and Christine Lindop

PAPL
DISCARDED

Wapiti regional library

RETOLD BY JENNIFER BASSETT

The Kiss

Love Stories from North America

Illustrated by
Alan Marks

OXFORD UNIVERSITY PRESS

OXFORD

UNIVERSITY PRESS

Great Clarendon Street, Oxford, OX2 6DP, United Kingdom

Oxford University Press is a department of the University of Oxford.
It furthers the University's objective of excellence in research, scholarship,
and education by publishing worldwide. Oxford is a registered trade
mark of Oxford University Press in the UK and in certain other countries

This simplified edition © Oxford University Press 2013

The moral rights of the author have been asserted

First published in Oxford Bookworms 2013

10 9 8 7 6 5 4 3 2 1

No unauthorized photocopying

All rights reserved. No part of this publication may be reproduced,
stored in a retrieval system, or transmitted, in any form or by any means,
without the prior permission in writing of Oxford University Press, or as
expressly permitted by law, by licence or under terms agreed with the
appropriate reprographics rights organization. Enquiries concerning
reproduction outside the scope of the above should be sent to the ELT
Rights Department, Oxford University Press, at the address above

You must not circulate this work in any other form and you must
impose this same condition on any acquirer

Links to third party websites are provided by Oxford in good faith and
for information only. Oxford disclaims any responsibility for the materials
contained in any third party website referenced in this work

ISBN: 978 0 19 478615 7

A complete recording of this Bookworms edition of
The Kiss: Love Stories from North America is available in an audio pack. ISBN: 978 0 19 478605 8

Printed in China

Word count (main text): 12,732

For more information on the Oxford Bookworms Library,
visit www.oup.com/bookworms

CONTENTS

NOTE ABOUT THE LANGUAGE

In these stories some of the characters use non-standard forms, for example: *ain't* instead of *am not* / *is not* / *are not*; and double negatives, as in *You never gave him no chance*. This is how the authors of the original stories represent the spoken language that their characters would use in real life. These non-standard forms are listed in the glossary on page 61.

The Kiss

Kate Chopin

It was still light out of doors, but inside with the curtains closed and with only a little light from the fire, the room was full of shadows.

Brantain sat in one of those shadows; the shadow had moved over him and he did not mind. The darkness made him feel brave enough to stare for as long as he liked at the girl who sat in the firelight.

She was very good-looking, with that fine, rich coloring often found in women with dark brown hair and brown eyes. She sat calmly, with her hands resting on the cat that lay sleeping on her knees. From time to time she sent a slow look into the shadow where the man sat. They were talking of unimportant things, which were clearly not the things they were thinking about. She knew that he loved her – a simple, honest man, not clever enough to hide his feelings, and with no wish to do so.

For the past two weeks, at every tea party and every dinner party, he had been always at her side. She was sure he would soon ask her to marry him, and she meant to accept him. Brantain was dull and not at all good-looking, but he was extraordinarily rich; and she liked and wanted the kind of life that a rich husband could give her.

During one of the pauses in their conversation about the last tea party and the next dinner party, the door opened and a young man entered. Brantain knew him well. The girl turned her face toward him, but did not realize that he had not seen Brantain. In three steps he was next to her chair, and bending over her – before she had any idea what he planned to do – he gave her a long, slow, burning kiss upon her lips.

Brantain slowly stood up. The girl stood up too, but quickly, and the young man stood between them, amused and embarrassed at the same time.

The young man stood between them, amused and embarrassed.

'I . . . I believe . . .' said Brantain uncomfortably, ' I . . . I see that I have stayed too long. I had no idea, that is, I must go, I . . . I must say goodbye.'

He was holding his hat with both hands, and probably did not see that she was holding out her hand to him. She was deeply embarrassed, and could not trust herself to speak.

'But I didn't see him sitting there, Nattie! I know it's very embarrassing for you. But I hope you'll forgive me this once. Why, what's the matter?'

'Don't touch me, don't come near me,' she replied angrily. 'What do you mean by it? Why did you enter the house without ringing?'

'I came in with your brother, as I often do,' he explained coldly. 'We came in the side way. He went upstairs and I came in here hoping to find you. The explanation is simple enough. It was just an accident, a mistake. But do say you forgive me, Nathalie,' he said in a softer voice.

'Forgive you! You don't know what you're talking about,' said the girl. 'Let me pass. I have no idea – yet – if I will ever forgive you or not.'

At that next dinner party which she and Brantain had talked about, she walked over to him with a wide smile but with a worried look in her fine eyes.

'Will you let me speak to you for a moment or two, Mr Brantain?' she asked in a soft voice.

He seemed deeply unhappy, but when she took his arm and walked away with him, searching for a quiet corner, a little hope brightened the misery on his face. She spoke out bravely.

'Perhaps it was wrong of me to ask you for this talk, Mr Brantain, but – but, oh, I have been very uncomfortable, almost miserable since that little meeting the other day. I wondered if you had misunderstood, and . . . and perhaps believed things . . .' Hope was beginning to win the battle over misery in Brantain's round, honest face. 'Of course, I know it means nothing to you, but I do want you to understand that Mr Harvy is a close friend of many years. Why, we have been almost like brother and sister, I may say. He is my brother's oldest, closest friend and he often behaves just like one of the family. Oh, I know it is so unnecessary to tell you this, it's of no interest to you at all,' she was almost crying now, 'but it makes so much difference to me what you . . . what you think of . . . of me.' Her voice was now very low and unhappy. The misery had all disappeared from Brantain's face.

'Then you do really care what I think, Miss Nathalie? May I call you Miss Nathalie?'

They turned into a long garden room at the side of the house, full of tall plants. They walked slowly to the very end of it. When they turned to walk back, Brantain's face shone with happiness, and hers shone with the light of victory.

Harvy was among the guests at the wedding, and he found her at a moment when she stood alone.

'Your husband,' he said smiling, 'has sent me over to kiss you.'

Her face flushed a deep pink.

'I suppose it's natural for a man to behave generously at his own wedding. He tells me he doesn't want his marriage to break the close friendship between you and me. I don't know what you've been telling him,' he said with an unpleasant smile, 'but he has sent me here to kiss you.'

She felt she was playing her game successfully; this is what she had planned and wanted. Her eyes were bright and tender with a smile as they looked up into his; and her lips looked hungry for the kiss which they invited.

'But, you know,' he went on quietly, 'I didn't tell him this because it would be ungrateful of me, but I can tell you. I've stopped kissing women; it's dangerous.'

Well, she had Brantain and his million dollars. A person can't have everything in this world, and it was a little unreasonable of her to ask for it.

The Bride Comes to Yellow Sky

Stephen Crane

The great Pullman coach of the California Express moved quietly and smoothly along the railway. It almost flew along. In fact, it seemed that the train itself was not traveling west, but that Texas was moving east past the train windows. Miles and miles of green grass, or brown and yellow rough ground, little groups of wooden houses, woods of tall young trees – all were traveling into the east, disappearing into the far distance behind the train.

A newly married pair had got into the Pullman at San Antonio. The man's face was reddened from many days in the wind and sun, and because of his new black clothes his red-brown hands were very noticeable every time he moved. He sat with a hand on each knee, like a man waiting to have his hair cut. From time to time he looked quickly and shyly at the other passengers, then looked away again.

The bride was not pretty, nor was she very young. She wore a blue dress, with a great many buttons here and there all over it. She could not stop looking at the buttons, and they seemed to embarrass her. It was clear that she had been a cook, and that she knew she would always be a cook, and that was fine. She had a calm, peaceful face, although it was a little flushed now because of the stares of the other passengers in the Pullman.

They were clearly very happy.

'Ever been in a Pullman before?' he asked, smiling.

'No,' she answered, 'I never was. It's fine, ain't it?'

'Great! And then after a while we'll go forward to the dining car and get a meal. Finest meal in the world. Costs a dollar.'

'Oh, does it?' cried the bride. 'Costs a dollar? Why, that's too much – for us – ain't it, Jack?'

'Not this trip,' he answered bravely. 'We're going to do everything.'

Later, he explained to her about the trains. 'You see, it's a thousand miles from one end of Texas to the other, and this train runs right across it and never stops but four times.'

He showed her the many wonderful things on the train – the shining glass and silver, the beautiful sea-green material on the seats, the dark shiny wood, the pictures on the walls and ceiling.

To the newly married pair, everything around them was as bright and wonderful as their marriage that morning in San Antonio. The man's face especially shone with happiness, which the black porter clearly found amusing. This porter watched them with a little smile all the time. He told them what to do and where to go, always very politely, but he seemed to enjoy giving them orders. The other passengers also seemed amused by them. What is it about newly married people that is so amusing? People have always laughed at them, and the passengers on this train were no different.

'We arrive in Yellow Sky at 3.42,' he said, looking fondly into her eyes.

'Oh, do we?' she said. Of course she knew this already,

but she was a new wife, and new wives like to please their husbands by showing surprise. She took from a pocket a little silver watch, and as she held it before her and stared at it carefully, the new husband's face shone.

'I bought it in San Antonio from a friend of mine,' he told her happily.

The waiters knew all about the newly married pair already.

'It's seventeen minutes past twelve,' she said, looking up at him with a shy, but playful, smile. Another passenger, seeing this smile, turned his head away to hide his own smile.

At last they went to the dining-car. Several black waiters in their white suits watched their entrance with interest. They knew all about the newly married pair already. One of the older waiters brought their food, and all through the meal he showed a fatherly care for them. It was all very polite. And yet, as the pair returned to their Pullman coach, they showed in their faces a feeling of escape.

To the left, miles down a long purple hillside, was the distant Rio Grande, and ahead of them was Yellow Sky, getting closer by the minute. And as they came closer, it was clear that the husband was becoming very restless. His great brown hands were moving around all the time; sometimes he did not even hear his bride when she spoke to him.

In fact, Jack Potter was beginning to find that the shadow of his marriage lay heavy upon him. He, the town marshal of Yellow Sky, was a man known, liked, and feared. He believed that he loved a girl, had gone to San Antonio to meet her, and had asked her to marry him – but he had not told Yellow Sky anything about it. He was now bringing his bride to a town who knew nothing about his marriage.

Of course, people in Yellow Sky married as they pleased, just like other people. But Potter was the town marshal, and town marshals cannot do as they please. He knew very well that his marriage was an important thing to his town. Only something like the burning of the new hotel would be more important. His friends would not forgive him.

He had wondered about sending a message or a letter, but he feared to do it. And now the train was hurrying him toward Yellow Sky, and the great surprise of its people.

He decided that he would make the journey from the station to his house as quickly and as secretly as he could. When safe at home, he could send out a message about his marriage, and then not go among the people until they had learnt to live with the idea.

The bride looked at him. 'What's worrying you, Jack?'

He laughed a little. 'I'm not worrying, girl. I'm only thinking of Yellow Sky.'

She understood him and flushed.

They looked at each other lovingly, with shining eyes, but they were both ashamed; both knew that Yellow Sky was coming. Potter often laughed the same nervous laugh. The flush on the bride's face did not go away.

Soon the porter came, calling out the name of Yellow Sky. He took their bag, and Potter found a coin in his pocket and gave it to him. He had seen others doing this, knew how it was done, but he was not comfortable doing it as it was new to him.

As the train began to slow, they moved to the end of the Pullman coach. Then the two engines and the long line of coaches pulled into the station of Yellow Sky.

'The train has to take water here,' said Potter. His voice was low and sad; he seemed to be talking about a death in the family. Before the train stopped, his eyes had looked up and down the station, and he was pleased and surprised to see that there was only one man at the far end of the platform. The train stopped, and the porter opened the door.

'Come on, girl,' said Potter. As he helped her down the steps, they each laughed nervously. He took the bag from the porter, and told his wife to hold his arm. As they walked quickly away, he saw along the platform that the man at the other end had turned and was running toward them, waving. Potter laughed even more nervously. The news of his marriage was arriving in Yellow Sky. He held his wife's arm, and they hurried away.

Behind them, the porter stood on the steps of the train, laughing foolishly.

• 2 •

The California Express on the Southern Railway was expected at Yellow Sky in twenty-one minutes. There were six men in the bar of the 'Weary Gentleman' saloon. One was a traveling salesman who talked a lot; three were Texans who did not care to talk at that time; and two were Mexican farm workers who did not usually talk in the 'Weary Gentleman' saloon. The barman's dog lay in front of the door, and he looked around sleepily all the time, with the watchfulness of a dog who is often kicked.

Across the sandy street there were some squares of bright green grass. Under the hot sun they seemed so wonderfully green next to the sands that burned near them. At the cooler end of the railway station a man without a coat sat on a chair and smoked his pipe. The Rio Grande circled around the town, and beyond the river were miles and miles of red-brown mesquite trees.

Except for the men in the 'Weary Gentleman' saloon, Yellow Sky was sleeping. The salesman, who was a newcomer to the town, sat by the bar talking and happily telling stories, knowing that nobody in Yellow Sky had heard his stories before.

He was in the middle of a long story about an old man, a desk, and some stairs, when a young man suddenly appeared in the open door. He cried:

'Scratchy Wilson's drunk, and is out in the town with a gun in each hand.'

At once the two Mexicans put down their glasses and disappeared quietly out of the back door of the saloon.

The salesman, knowing nothing about Scratchy Wilson, answered, 'All right, old man. Suppose he is. Come in and have a drink, anyhow.'

But the information had hit everyone in the room hard, and the salesman began to realize its importance. Everybody had become very serious.

'Say,' he said, puzzled, 'what is this?'

The three Texans got ready to speak, but the young man at the door was before them.

'It means, my friend,' he answered, as he came into the saloon, 'that for the next two hours this town won't be a healthy place to be.'

The barman went to the door and locked it. Reaching out of the window, he pulled in heavy wooden shutters and locked them too. Immediately the bar became a different place, dark and shadowy. The salesman was looking from one man to another.

'But, say,' he cried, 'what is this, anyhow? You don't mean there's going to be a gun-fight?'

'Don't know if there'll be a fight or not,' answered one man darkly. 'But there'll be some shootin' – some good shootin'.'

The young man who had warned them waved his hand. 'Oh, there'll be a fight fast enough if anyone wants it.

*'Scratchy Wilson's drunk, and is out in the town
with a gun in each hand.'*

Anybody can get a fight out there in the street. There's a fight just waiting.'

The salesman had a stranger's interest in things, but he was also now beginning to be afraid for himself.

'What did you say his name was?' he asked.

'Scratchy Wilson,' they answered together.

'And will he kill anybody? What are you going to do? Does this happen often? Does he go crazy like this once a week or so? Can he break down that door?'

'No, he can't break down that door,' replied the barman. 'He's tried it three times. But when he comes, make sure to lie down on the floor, stranger. He's sure to shoot at it, and a bullet may come through.'

After that the salesman kept a very careful eye on the door. The time had not yet come to lie down on the floor, but in order to be ready for it, he moved closer to the wall.

'Will he kill anybody?' he said again.

The men laughed at his foolish question.

'He's out to shoot, and he's out for trouble. Don't see any good in tryin' to find out.'

'But what do you do when this happens? What do you do?'

A man replied, 'Why, he and Jack Potter—'

'But,' the other men said together, 'Jack Potter's in San Antonio.'

'Well, who is he? What's he got to do with it?'

'Oh, he's the town marshal. He goes out and fights Scratchy when he goes crazy like this.'

'Wow,' said the salesman. 'Nice job he's got.'

The voices were now just whispers. The salesman became more and more puzzled and nervous, and wished to ask more questions. But when he tried, the men just looked at him angrily and made signs at him to keep silent.

The silence of waiting was upon them. In the deep shadows of the room their eyes shone as they listened for sounds from the street. One man held up three fingers to the barman, and the barman, moving like a ghost, gave him a glass and a bottle. The man filled the glass with whiskey, and put the bottle down noiselessly. He drank the whiskey straight down, and turned again toward the door in silence. The salesman saw that the barman, without a sound, had taken a Winchester rifle from under the bar. Then he whispered to the salesman:

'You come here with me, back of the bar.'

'No, thanks,' whispered the salesman nervously. 'I'll stay here where I can run for the back door.'

The barman called him again. The salesman obeyed, and found himself seated on a box with his head below the top of the bar. He saw that there was a lot of metal behind the bar, which would be between him and a bullet, and this comforted him greatly. The barman sat on a box next to him.

'You see,' he whispered, 'this here Scratchy Wilson is a wonder with a gun, and when he goes out lookin' for a fight, we all hide – naturally. He's crazy when he's drunk. When he's not drunk, he's all right – kind of simple – wouldn't hurt a fly – nicest guy in town. But when he's drunk – whoo!'

Everyone was still for a time. 'I wish Jack Potter was back

from San Antonio,' said the barman. 'He shot Wilson up once – in the leg. He'd come in here and get things straight.'

A little later they heard from a distance the sound of a shot, followed by three wild yells. The men in the darkened saloon moved a little and looked at each other.

'Here he comes,' they said.

• 3 •

A man in a dark red shirt came round a corner and walked into the middle of the main street of Yellow Sky. In either hand the man held a long, heavy, blue-black revolver. Often

From time to time he shouted out his crazy warnings.

he yelled, and these cries seemed too loud to be just a man's voice. They rang over the roofs of a seemingly empty town, beating against walls of silence.

The man's boots had red tops with little bits of gold on them. His face burned with a fury born of whiskey, and his eyes searched the still doorways and windows, looking for enemies to fight. He walked softly, like a midnight cat. From time to time he shouted out his crazy warnings. The long revolvers were easy in his hands, moving faster than light at any sign of trouble. In that still, calm street the only sounds were his terrible invitations.

There was no offer of fight; no offer of fight. The man called to the sky. There were no answering calls. He yelled and shouted and moved his revolvers here and everywhere.

The dog of the barman of the 'Weary Gentleman' saloon had not heard the news of the day. He still lay sleeping in front of the door to the bar. When he saw the dog, the man lifted his revolver, in an amused kind of way. When he saw the man, the dog jumped up and walked away, with his head low, and growling. The man yelled, and the dog began to run. As it turned a corner, there was a loud noise, and something hit the ground just in front of it. The dog screamed, turned, and ran fast the other way. Again there was a sharp noise, and a little cloud of sand was kicked into the air. The dog, crazy with fear, turned this way and that way. The man stood laughing, his revolvers at his sides.

Finally, the man noticed the closed door of the 'Weary Gentleman' saloon. He went to it, and banging on the door with a revolver, yelled for a drink.

The door stayed shut. The man picked up a bit of paper from the street and fixed it to the door with his knife. Then he walked to the opposite side of the street, turned quickly and smoothly, and fired at the bit of paper. He missed it by one centimeter. He shouted angrily, and went away. Later, he comfortably rained bullets on the windows of his closest friend. The man was playing games with this town.

But still there was no offer of fight. The name of Jack Potter, his old enemy, came into his head, and he thought it would be a pleasant thing to go to Potter's house and make him come out and fight. He began to walk there, singing a wild battle song as he went.

When he arrived, Potter's house had the same still front as all the other houses. The man shouted out his invitation to battle. The house, unmoved, looked down on him silently. It gave no sign. The man waited a little, then shouted more invitations to battle, using some wonderful adjectives.

Then came a strange thing to watch – a man going crazy with fury, because of the stillness of a house. He was like a wild winter wind blowing down from the north; he was the noise of two hundred Mexicans fighting. From time to time, he stopped for air, or to reload his revolvers.

• 4 •

Potter and his bride walked quickly, with their heads held low. Sometimes they laughed together, a secret, ashamed little laugh.

'Next corner, dear,' he said finally.

They walked more quickly. Potter had just lifted his hand

to show his bride her new home when, as they came round the corner, they came face to face with a man in a dark red shirt who was hurriedly pushing bullets into a large revolver. At once the man dropped his revolver to the ground, and, quicker than light, pulled out his other revolver. It was aimed straight at Jack Potter's heart.

There was silence. Potter's tongue turned to stone in his mouth. He freed his arm from the woman's hand, and he dropped the bag to the ground. The bride's face had gone as yellow as old paper. Her frightened eyes stared at the man with the gun.

The two men looked at each other, with only two meters between them. The man with the revolver smiled with a new and quiet fury.

'Tried to sneak up on me,' he said. 'Tried to sneak up on me!' His eyes grew wilder. As Potter made a small movement, the man pushed his revolver furiously into Potter's face.

'No, don't you do it, Jack Potter. Don't you move a finger toward a gun just yet. Don't you move at all. The time has come for me to finish with you, and I'm goin' to do it my own way. So if you don't want a bullet in you, just mind what I tell you.'

Potter looked at his enemy. 'I ain't got a gun on me, Scratchy,' he said. 'Honest, I ain't.'

His body was getting itself ready to fight, but in his head was a picture of the Pullman, the shining glass and silver, the beautiful sea-green material on the seats, the dark shiny wood – all the wonderful things that belonged to his

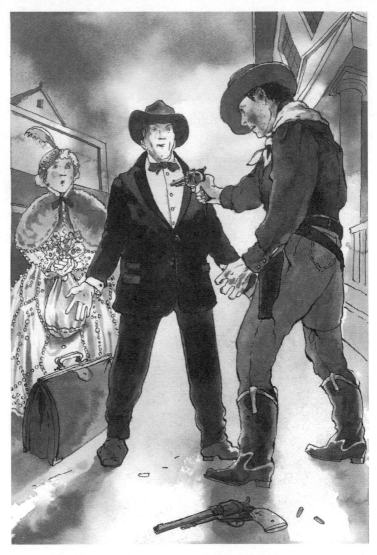

'I ain't got a gun on me,' said Potter. 'You'll have to do all the shootin' yourself.'

marriage and his new life as a husband. He spoke again to his enemy.

'You know I fight when it comes to fightin', Scratchy Wilson, but I ain't got a gun on me. You'll have to do all the shootin' yourself.'

His enemy's face turned purple with fury. He stepped forward and waved his revolver in front of Potter's chest.

'Don't you tell me you ain't got no gun on you, you dog. Don't tell me no lie like that. There ain't a man in Texas ever seen you without no gun. Don't take me for no kid.' His eyes burned with a furious light.

'I ain't taking you for no kid,' answered Potter. His feet had not moved an inch backward. 'I'm takin' you for a crazy fool. I tell you I ain't got a gun, and I ain't. If you're goin' to shoot me up, why don't you begin now? You'll never get a chance like this again.'

These reasonable words began to make Wilson calmer. He spoke more quietly. 'If you ain't got a gun, why ain't you got a gun?' he said unpleasantly. 'Been to church?'

'I ain't got a gun because I've just come from San Antonio with my wife. I'm married,' said Potter. 'I wasn't plannin' on meetin' crazy guys like you sneakin' around when I brought my wife home. But I sure wish I had my gun on me now.'

'Married!' said Scratchy, not understanding at all.

'Yes, married. I'm married,' said Potter clearly.

'Married?' said Scratchy. Seemingly for the first time he saw the frightened woman at the other man's side. 'No!' he said. A sudden window into another world had opened for him. He took a step backward, and his arm with the revolver dropped to his side. 'Is this the lady?' he asked.

'Yes, this is the lady,' answered Potter.

There was another long silence.

'Well,' said Wilson at last, slowly, 'I s'pose it's all off now.'

'It's all off if you say so, Scratchy. You know I didn't make the trouble.' Potter lifted his bag.

'Well, I s'pose it's gotta be off, Jack,' said Wilson. He was looking at the ground. 'Married!'

He did not feel a special kindness toward women; it was simply that the idea of marriage was new to him and he did not know how to behave. He picked up his other revolver from the ground, and placing both guns in their holsters, he went away. His feet made long boat-shaped marks in the sandy ground.

A Seashore Wooing

Lucy Maud Montgomery

Fir Cottage, Plover Sands. July Sixth

We arrived here late last night, and all day Aunt Martha has stayed in her room to rest. So I had to stay in my room and rest too, although I was not at all tired and really wanted to go out and enjoy myself.

My name is Marguerite Forrester – an impossibly long name for so small a girl. Aunt Martha does not like my name, but she always uses it in full. Connie Shelmardine used to call me Rita. Connie was my best friend last year at school. We write to each other sometimes, but Aunt Martha does not approve of this.

I have always lived with Aunt Martha – my parents died when I was a baby. Aunt Martha says that all her money will come to me when she dies – but only if I please her. This means – but, oh, you do not know what 'pleasing' Aunt Martha means.

Aunt is a real man-hater. Actually, she doesn't like women much either, and she trusts nobody except Mrs Saxby, her maid. I like Mrs Saxby. She's not as stony-hearted as Aunt, although she gets a little stonier every year. I suppose I shall soon start to become stony myself, but it hasn't happened yet. My blood is still unreasonably warm and I feel full of life, which gets me into trouble.

Aunt Martha's heart will stop beating if she ever sees me talking to a man. She watches me closely, wanting to guard me from those wild and dangerous creatures called men. So I have to walk quietly and pretend to be good, even if I am not. And all the time I have the wildest dreams of being bad.

We have come down to spend a few weeks at Fir Cottage. Our good landlady, Mrs Blake, is a large, kindly person, and I think she likes me. I have been talking away to her all day, because there are times when I absolutely must talk to someone or go mad.

July Tenth

This kind of life is extraordinarily dull. Every day is the same. I go to the beach with Aunt Martha and Mrs Saxby in the morning, read to Aunt in the afternoons, and sit around miserably by myself in the evenings. Mrs Blake has lent me a very fine spyglass which she owns. She says her husband brought it home from abroad before he died.

While Aunt and Mrs Saxby walk slowly up and down the beach, leaving me free, I amuse myself by looking through the spyglass and seeing distant seas and coasts. In this way I can take a look into a forbidden world. We see few people, although there is a large summer hotel about a mile up the beach. Our part of the beach does not seem to be popular with the hotel guests – they prefer the rocks and do not come down to our end. This pleases Aunt Martha greatly.

On our first morning here I noticed something white on the rocks, about half a mile away, and turned my spyglass on it. There – and it looked only a stone's throw away from me – was a young man. He was lying on a rock, looking dreamily out to sea. There was something about his face that reminded me of someone, but I could not think who it was.

Every morning since we arrived five days ago, he has appeared on the same rock. He seems to be a person who likes to be by himself. It's a good thing that Aunt doesn't know what I am watching through my spyglass. What *would* she say?

July Eleventh

I shall have to stop looking into the forbidden world, I'm afraid. This morning I turned my spyglass, as usual, on to his favorite rock. I nearly fell over in my surprise, because he was also looking through a spyglass straight at me, it seemed. How foolish I felt! But after a few minutes I just had to have another look, just to see what he was doing. Then he calmly put down his spyglass, stood up, lifted his hat, and bowed politely to me – or at least, in my direction. I dropped my spyglass and smiled, feeling amused and foolish at the same time. Then I remembered that he was probably watching me again, and maybe he was thinking that my smile was for him. I stopped smiling at once, shut my spyglass, and did not touch it again. Soon after we came home.

July Twelfth

Something has happened at last. Today I went to the shore as usual, and I had decided absolutely not to look at him or at that end of the beach at all. But in the end I had to take a quick look, and saw him on the rocks with his spyglass looking at me. When he saw that I was looking, he put down the spyglass, held out his hands, and began to spell out something in the deaf-mute alphabet. Connie taught it to me last year because we wanted to talk secretly across the classroom. I gave one frightened look at Aunt Martha's back, and then watched him while he spelled:

'I am Francis Shelmardine. Aren't you Miss Forrester, my sister's friend?'

Francis Shelmardine! Now I knew who he reminded me of. I have heard endless talk from Connie on this wonderful

I saw him on the rocks with his spyglass looking at me.

brother of hers, Francis the clever, Francis the good-looking, Francis this, and Francis that. In fact, he has always been the young man who appears in my dreams. It was too wonderful. I just stared back at him through my spyglass.

'May we know each other?' he went on. 'May I come over and introduce myself? Right hand, yes; left hand, no.'

Oh dear! He mustn't come here. *What* would happen? Sadly, I waved my left hand. He looked very disappointed as he spelled out:

'Why not? Would your friends disapprove?'

I spelled back: 'Yes.'

'Are you unhappy because I asked you?' was his next question.

What had happened to all Aunt Martha's careful teaching? I am embarrassed to say that I lifted my left hand shyly. I just had time to see his pleased smile before Aunt Martha came up and said it was time to go home. So I stood up, shook the sand from my dress, and obediently followed my good aunt home.

July Thirteenth

When we went to the shore this morning, I was so nervous and worried. I had to wait until Aunt got tired of reading and set off along the shore with Mrs Saxby. Then I reached for my spyglass.

Mr Shelmardine and I had a long conversation. With the deaf-mute alphabet we did not want to talk around things uselessly. So we used as few words as possible, and our conversation went something like this:

'You're not angry with me?'

'No – but I should be.'

'Why?'

'It is wrong to deceive Aunt.'

'I am not a dangerous person.'

'That is not the question.'

'Is it not possible to change the way she thinks?'

'Absolutely not.'

'Mrs Allardyce, who is staying at the hotel, knows her well. Shall I bring her over to explain that I'm not a bad person?'

'It won't do a bit of good.'

'Then it is hopeless.'

'Yes.'

'Suppose you were free to do what you liked . . . Would you refuse to know me then?'

'No.'

'Do you ever come to the shore alone?'

'No. Aunt does not permit me.'

'Must she know?'

'Yes. I don't like to go out if she doesn't permit it.'

'You will not refuse to talk with me like this sometimes?'

'I don't know. Perhaps not.'

I had to go home then. As we went, Mrs Saxby told me that my face had a nice healthy colour. Aunt Martha looked very disapproving. If I'm ever really ill, I know she will spend her last cent to help me. But she doesn't really like to see me enjoying life. She prefers to see me quiet and pale in this sad life.

July Seventeenth

I have 'talked' many times with Mr Shelmardine in these past four days. He is staying here for several more weeks. This morning his message sent from the rocks was this:

'I plan to see you at last. Tomorrow I will walk over and pass you.'

'You must not. Aunt will wonder what is going on.'

'No danger. Don't worry. I will do nothing foolish.'

I suppose he will come. He seems to want to very much. Of course, I cannot stop him walking up and down on our end of the beach all day if he chooses. But if he does, Aunt will just go away and not come back here at all.

I wonder what I should wear tomorrow.

July Nineteenth

Yesterday morning Aunt Martha was happy and peaceful. It is terrible of me to deceive her like this and I do feel bad about it. I sat down on the sand and pretended to read a book called *The Story of the Church in Africa* – Aunt approves of books like that. I was so nervous!

In a while Aunt said loudly: 'Marguerite, there is a man coming this way. We will move down the beach.'

And we moved. Poor Aunt!

Mr Shelmardine came bravely on. I felt my heart beating right to the end of my fingers. He stopped by the old fishing boat, lying on its side in the sand. Aunt had turned her back on him.

I lifted my head from my book and took a quick look. He lifted his hat with a smile in his eyes. Just then Aunt said, icily: 'We will go home, Marguerite. That person clearly plans to push himself in here.'

And so, home we came.

This morning he 'spoke' by alphabet from the rocks: 'Letter from Connie. Message for you. I'm going to give it to you myself. Do you ever go to church?'

Now, at home I go to church every week. But Aunt Martha and Mrs Saxby do not like the church here at Plover Sands, and will not even go in through the door. And of course, I am not permitted to go either. But it was impossible to explain all this by the alphabet, so I just replied: 'Not here.'

'Will you not go tomorrow morning?'

'Aunt will not let me.'

'Talk to her nicely.'

'Talking nicely never does any good. She doesn't listen.'

'Suppose Mrs Allardyce calls and offers to take you to church with her?'

I *have* said Mrs Allardyce's name during a conversation with Aunt, and I have discovered that she disapproves of Mrs Allardyce. So I said:

'It will be useless. I will ask Aunt to let me go to church, but I feel almost sure that she will not permit me.'

This evening Aunt was unusually kind, so I was brave enough to ask her.

'Marguerite,' she said seriously, 'you know that I do not go to church here.'

'But, Aunt,' I went on, nervously, 'couldn't I go alone? It is not very far – and I will be very careful.'

Aunt just gave me a look which said about forty different things, and I was turning away in misery when Mrs Saxby – wonderful Mrs Saxby – said:

'I really think there would be no danger in letting the child go to church.'

Aunt gave me a look which said about forty different things.

Aunt always listens to what Mrs Saxby says, and so she looked at me, and said: 'Well, I will think about it and let you know in the morning, Marguerite.'

I do hope that Aunt Martha has a very good night's sleep, and wakes up feeling that the world is a pleasant place.

July Twentieth

This morning was a beautiful warm day, and after breakfast Aunt said: 'I think you may go to church if you wish, Marguerite. Remember that you must be careful, and quiet, and polite, and not speak to any strangers.'

I ran upstairs and found my prettiest dress. It is a lovely soft gray with shiny bits in it. Every time I get any new clothes, Aunt Martha and I have a terrible battle. I think she would like me to wear dresses and hats that were fashionable a hundred years ago. Connie always says that my clothes are very nice and interestingly different from other people's. That's what Connie thinks – I don't agree.

But *I* chose this dress and it is really very pretty. I wore a little silvery-gray hat, with some pale pink flowers on it, and I pinned to my dress some of the sweetest little pink roses from the garden. Then I ran downstairs for Aunt Martha to look at me.

'Really, child,' she said, disapprovingly, 'you have dressed yourself up for a summer lunch party, it seems to me.'

'But, Aunty,' I said, 'I'm all in gray – every bit of me.'

Aunt Martha turned her mouth down at the corners. That face says about a hundred different disapproving things. But I walked off to church like a singing bird.

In the church I saw Mr Shelmardine at once. He was sitting right across from me, and there was a smile in his eyes. I did not look at him again. I was careful, and quiet, and polite, and not even looking at anybody.

When church was finished, he waited for me at the door. I pretended not to see him until he said, 'Good morning,' in a lovely deep voice. It was the kind of voice that you could listen to for ever. You felt it could be a very gentle voice too. When we went down the steps, he took my book, and we walked together up the long country road.

'Thank you so much for coming today,' he said.

'It was very difficult to make Aunt Martha agree to it,' I said. 'Mrs Saxby helped – she made it possible for me.'

'I don't know Mrs Saxby, but I like her very much already,' he said warmly. 'But is there any way we can persuade your aunt that it's all right for us to meet? I will do anything to make that happen.'

'There is none. Aunt Martha is very good and kind to me, but she will never stop trying to take care of me. She will go on doing it until I'm fifty. And she hates men!'

Mr Shelmardine looked serious, and began to hit the poor wild flowers at the side of the road with his walking stick.

'Then there is no hope that I can see you openly and honestly,' he said.

'Not at this time,' I said in a whisper.

We were silent for a while, and then began to talk of other things. He told me how he first saw me.

'I saw these people who were always on the beach in the same place at the same time, and I wanted to know who they were. So one day I took my spyglass. I could see you very clearly. You were reading and had your hat off. I asked Mrs Allardyce who were the people staying in Fir Cottage, and she told me. I had heard Connie talk about you, and I decided to try and meet you.'

When we reached the path going to Fir Cottage, I held out my hand for my book.

'You mustn't come any closer, Mr Shelmardine,' I said hurriedly. 'I don't want Aunt to see you.'

He took my hand and held it, looking at me seriously.

'Suppose tomorrow I walk up to the cottage and ask for you?'

'Oh! Please don't!' I said miserably. 'Aunt Martha will – but you're not serious, are you?'

'I suppose not,' he said sadly. 'Of course I won't do anything that will make life unpleasant for you. But this must not be our last meeting.'

'Aunt won't permit me to come to church again,' I said.

'Does she ever have a sleep in the afternoons?' he asked.

I drew a little circle on the sandy path with the toe of my right shoe.

'Sometimes.'

'I shall be at the old fishing boat on the beach tomorrow afternoon at two-thirty,' he said.

I pulled my hand away from his.

'I couldn't – you know I couldn't,' I cried – and then my face flushed up to my ears.

'Are you sure you couldn't?' He moved his head a little closer to mine.

'Absolutely sure,' I whispered.

At last he gave me my book back.

'Will you give me a rose?'

I unpinned all the little roses and gave them to him. He lifted them until they touched his lips. As for me, I ran up the path with my heart beating wildly. At the corner I looked back. He was still standing there with his hat off.

July Twenty-fourth

On Monday afternoon I left the cottage secretly and went down to the beach. Aunt Martha and Mrs Saxby were having their usual afternoon sleep and I was supposed to be reading my book about the church in my room.

Mr Shelmardine was standing by the old fishing boat, but he came quickly across the sand to meet me.

'This is very kind of you,' he said.

'I should not be here,' I said. 'But it is so lonely there – and I can't read books about the church *all* the time.'

Mr Shelmardine laughed. 'Mr and Mrs Allardyce are on the other side of the boat. Will you come and meet them?'

How nice of him to bring them! I knew I would like Mrs Allardyce, just because Aunt Martha didn't. We had a lovely walk. I never thought of the time until Mr Shelmardine said it was four o'clock.

'Oh, is it as late as that?' I cried. 'I must go at once.'

'I'm sorry we have kept you so long,' said Mr Shelmardine in a worried voice. 'What will happen, if your aunt is awake?'

'It's too terrible to think about,' I said seriously. 'I'm sorry, Mr Shelmardine, but you mustn't come with me.'

*'Mr Shelmardine!' I said. 'You shouldn't put these ideas
into my head.'*

'We will be here tomorrow afternoon,' he said.

'Mr Shelmardine!' I said. 'You shouldn't put these ideas into my head. They won't come out – not even if I read six books about the church from beginning to end.'

We looked at each other for a second. Then he began to smile, and we both started laughing.

'Let me know if your aunt is angry with you,' he called after me as I ran away up the path.

But Aunt Martha was not awake – and I have been to the beach three afternoons since then. I was there today, and I'm going tomorrow for a boat trip with Mr Shelmardine and the Allardyces. But I'm afraid he will do something foolish soon. Today he said: 'I don't think I can do this any longer.'

'Do what?' I asked.

'You know very well,' he answered. 'Meeting you in this secretive way, and making you worried and miserable about your aunt. I don't want it to be like this. It's only because your aunt is so unreasonable that I meet you like this.'

'I'm sorry,' I whispered.

'No, *you* mustn't be sorry,' he said seriously. 'But I think I must go honestly to your aunt and tell her everything.'

'You'll never see me again if you do that,' I said quickly – and then wished I hadn't said it.

'That is the most frightening thing you could say,' he said.

July Twenty-fifth

It is all over, and I am the most miserable girl in the world. Aunt Martha has discovered everything, and it is right that I am punished for my wrong-doing.

I left secretly again this afternoon and went for that boat trip. We had a lovely time but we were very late getting in, and I hurried home very nervously. Aunt Martha met me at the door.

My dress was dirty from the boat, my hat was not straight, and my hair was wild and all over the place. I did not look at all like a good, careful, quiet girl, and I'm sure my face looked very ashamed. Aunt gave me a long, hard look and then followed me silently up to my room.

'Marguerite, what does this mean?'

I am not a good person, but I have never told lies. I told Aunt everything – well, almost everything. I didn't tell her about the spyglasses and the deaf-mute alphabet. She didn't ask me how I first met Mr Shelmardine. She just listened in stony, angry silence. I thought she would be furious with me, but it seemed that she couldn't even speak to me. I was too bad for words.

When I had finished, she stood up, gave me one furious stare, and left the room. A few minutes later Mrs Saxby came in, looking worried.

'My dear child, what have you been doing? Your aunt says that we are going home on the afternoon train tomorrow. She is terribly unhappy about something.'

I just lay on my bed and cried, while Mrs Saxby packed my suitcase. I will have no chance to explain to Mr Shelmardine. And I will never see him again, because Aunt will probably take me away to Africa or somewhere. He will just think I am a foolish, empty-headed girl. Oh, I am so unhappy!

July Twenty-sixth

I am the happiest girl in the world! How things have changed since yesterday. We leave Fir Cottage in an hour, but that doesn't matter any more.

I did not sleep for a second last night, and went miserably down to breakfast. Aunt did not speak to me or look at me, but to my surprise she told Mrs Saxby that she wanted to take a last walk on the beach. I knew they would take me too, to guard me from danger, and my heart was suddenly full of hope. Aunt knew nothing about the messages sent and received by spyglass.

I quietly followed my two guards to the beach and sat miserably on the sand while they went for their walk. Francis was on the rocks. When Aunt Martha and Mrs Saxby were at a safe distance, I began my message:

'All discovered. Aunt is very angry. We go home today.'

Then I quickly looked through my spyglass. His face showed real unhappiness. He replied:

'I must see you before you go.'

'Impossible. Aunt will never forgive me. Goodbye.'

I saw his face change. He had decided something very important, I could see. Nothing, nothing could make me put down my spyglass now – not even forty Aunt Marthas standing right behind me.

'I love you. You know it. Do you care for me? I must have my answer now.'

What a thing to happen! No time or chance to pretend to be shy or nervous or ask for time or anything like that. Aunt and Mrs Saxby had almost reached the place where they turned and walked back. I had just time to spell out my answer – 'Yes' – and read his answer.

'I shall go home at once, get Mother and Connie, follow you, and ask for my future wife. I shall win the battle. Have no fear. Until then, goodbye, my sweet love.'

'Marguerite,' said Mrs Saxby close to me. 'It is time to go.'

I got up obediently. Aunt Martha was as stony-faced as ever, and Mrs Saxby looked like a rainy day, but do you think I cared? I slowed down and walked behind them just once before we left the beach. I knew he was watching me, and I waved my hand.

I suppose I am really engaged to Mr Shelmardine. But was there ever a stranger wooing? And *what* will Aunt Martha say?

A White Heron

Sarah Orne Jewett

The woods were already filled with shadows one June evening, just before eight o'clock, although a bright sun, low in the west, still shone through the trees. A little girl was driving home her cow, a slow-moving, annoying creature, but also a good companion among the shadowy trees. Their way home was deep in the woods, but their feet knew the path very well, so the darkness did not matter.

It often took a long time to find the cow before Sylvia could bring her home. The cow seemed to enjoy hiding among the bushes. She wore a loud bell around her neck, but the clever creature had discovered that the bell did not ring if she stood very still. Luckily, the cow gave good milk and lots of it, so her owners did not mind about her hiding. And Sylvia had all the time in the world, and very little to do in that time except chase the cow.

The cow had now decided she wanted to go home, and stepped along the path more quickly. Sylvia wondered what her grandmother would say, because they were very late. It was a long time since she had left home at half-past five. But Mrs Tilley had chased the cow herself on many summer evenings and knew how difficult the old cow could be. She also knew that Sylvia loved being outside in the woods and fields. It was a great change for a little girl who had lived for eight years in a crowded noisy town full of factories.

Old Mrs Tilley had chosen Sylvia from her daughter's

houseful of children, to come and live with her at the farm. Sylvia was 'afraid of people', her mother said, but Mrs Tilley just laughed. 'I guess she won't be troubled much with people up at the old place!'

So the old grandmother took Sylvia away. And when at last they reached the door of the lonely farmhouse, and the cat came to walk around their legs purring loudly, Sylvia whispered that this was a beautiful place to live in, and she would never wish to go home.

That was a year ago, and now the girl and the cow followed the shadowy path through the woods. The cow stopped to drink in a little river, and Sylvia stood still and waited, letting her feet cool themselves in the shallow water. Up above her, in the great branches of the tall trees, the leaves moved gently in a little wind, and the birds were singing, preparing for the night. Sylvia herself felt sleepy, but it was not far to the house now, and the air was soft and sweet. She felt that she belonged in this quiet world of gray shadows and moving leaves, and her life in the noisy town seemed far away.

Suddenly the little woods-girl heard a clear whistle not far away. Not a bird's whistle, which is a friendly sound, but a boy's whistle – loud and strong and full of fight. Frightened, Sylvia tried to hide behind some bushes, but she was just too late. The enemy had discovered her, and called out in a friendly voice, 'Hallo, little girl, how far is it to the road?'

'A good long way,' answered Sylvia in a frightened little whisper. She was not brave enough to look at the tall young man, who carried a gun over his shoulder, but she came out from behind her bush and again followed the cow. The young man walked along beside her.

'I have been hunting for some birds,' the stranger said, 'and I have lost my way, and need a friend very much. Don't be afraid,' he added gently. 'Speak up, and tell me what your name is. And do you think I can spend the night at your house, and go out hunting early in the morning?'

'I have lost my way, and need a friend very much,' said the stranger.

Sylvia was more frightened than ever. What would her grandmother say about this? She did not know what to do and looked down at the ground. In the end she managed to whisper, 'Sylvy', when the young man again asked her name.

Mrs Tilley was at the door when the three companions arrived. The cow gave a loud moo to explain matters.

'Yes, you ought to be sorry!' Mrs Tilley said to the cow. 'Where was she hidin' herself this time, Sylvy?' But Sylvia kept silent, not knowing how to explain the stranger.

The young man put his gun by the door, and dropped his hunting bag next to it. He said good evening to Mrs Tilley, told his story, and asked for a night's rest at the farm.

'Put me anywhere you like,' he said. 'I must be off early in the morning, before day; but I am very hungry indeed. You can give me some milk, that's clear.'

'Oh yes, we can give you milk,' said Mrs Tilley. 'And you're welcome to what we've got. I'll milk the cow right now, an' you make yourself at home. There's plenty o' comfortable places to sleep round the farm,' she added kindly. 'Now step round an' put out a plate for the gentleman, Sylvy!'

Sylvia disappeared at once, pleased to have something to do, and she was hungry herself.

The young man was surprised to find this clean and comfortable little house in the New England wilderness. He had stayed in very different kinds of homes, where the chickens lived in the same room as the family. He listened with interest to the old woman talking, he watched Sylvia's pale face and shining gray eyes, and he said it was the best supper that he had eaten in a month. Afterward, the new friends sat in the doorway together while the moon came up.

'I've buried four children,' Mrs Tilley told the young man. 'Sylvy's mother and one son are all the children that I have now. Dan, my boy, was a great hunter, he was always out in the woods. Sylvy is like him, she knows all the woods an' fields, every tree an' bush. The wild creatures think she's one o' them. The squirrels will come and eat right out o' her hands, and all kinds o' birds. She knows all o' them. Just like Dan. He's been gone for years,' she said sadly. 'Dan an' his father, they didn't get along.'

There was some family sadness hidden in those words, but the young man did not hear it; he was too interested in something else.

'So Sylvy knows all about birds, does she?' he said. He looked round at the little girl who sat, shy and sleepy, in the moonlight. 'I've been collecting birds myself, ever since I was a boy.' (Mrs Tilley smiled.) 'But there are two or three unusual ones that I haven't found yet.'

'Do you put them in cages?' asked Mrs Tilley.

'Oh no, they're stuffed. And I've shot or caught every one myself. I saw a white heron two days ago, and I've been following it. The little white heron, it is,' and he turned to look at Sylvia, hoping that she had seen it. 'A strange tall white bird with soft feathers and long thin legs. Its nest is made of sticks, often in the top of a high tree.'

Sylvia's heart gave a wild beat. She knew that strange white bird, and had once got close to where it stood in the green marsh grass, over at the other side of the woods.

'I'd like to find that heron's nest more than anything,' the young man said. 'I'd give ten dollars to anybody who could show it to me,' he added, 'and I plan to spend the rest of my vacation hunting for it.'

The new friends sat in the doorway together while the moon came up.

Mrs Tilley listened to all this with amused interest, but Sylvia was watching the moonlight dancing in the trees. It was impossible to decide, during that night, how many wonderful things those ten dollars could buy.

The next day the young hunter walked around the woods, and Sylvia went with him. She had lost her fear of the young man, who was friendly and kind. He told her many things about the birds and where they lived and what they did. And he gave her a pocket-knife, which was a wonderful thing to her. She liked him very much indeed, but she did not like the shooting. She could not understand why he killed the birds that he seemed to love so much. But as the day passed, Sylvia still watched the young man, and the woman's heart, asleep in the child, slowly began to learn the dream of love. Together they stepped softly through the woodlands. They stopped to listen to a bird's song, then went forward, carefully moving branches to one side. They spoke little, and only in whispers; the young man going first and Sylvia following, with her gray eyes dark with excitement.

She was sad because they did not find the white heron, the bird that the young man wanted so much. But Sylvia only followed where he went; she could never speak first. It was hard enough for her to whisper 'yes' or 'no' to answer questions. At last evening came, and they found and drove the cow home together. And Sylvia smiled happily when they came to the place where she heard the whistle and was afraid only the night before.

Half a mile from home, at the far edge of the woods, on high ground, a great pine-tree stood. It was the last tree of an older forest, and around it a new wood of younger trees had grown. But the old pine-tree's head stood high above them all, and was seen from miles away across land and sea.

Sylvia knew this tree well. She believed that at the top it was possible to see the Atlantic Ocean. The little girl had never seen the sea, but she had often dreamed about it. Now, she had a new idea, which filled her with excitement. From the top of this great tree she could see all the world. So couldn't she also see where the white heron flew, where it came from, and where it went to? She would see where it flew into the trees, and she would remember the place, and find the hidden nest.

What an adventure it would be! And how wonderful, later in the morning, when she could tell her great secret!

The young hunter and the old grandmother slept deeply that night, but Sylvia lay awake, waiting for the short summer night to pass, and her great adventure to begin.

Before daylight, she quietly left the house and followed the path through the woods. The birds were making their first sleepy little calls, but Sylvia was thinking only about the great change that had come into her dull little life. Ah, Sylvy, Sylvy, do not forget that the birds and animals of the forest were your first friends!

Now she came to the great pine-tree, and small and foolish Sylvia began to climb. First, she must climb the white oak tree next to the pine-tree. She had often climbed this tree, and knew that one of its high branches went into the pine-tree, and she could move from one tree to the other. She made that dangerous crossing safely, and now began to climb the pine-tree itself, using all her fingers and toes to hold on. The way was harder than she thought; she must reach far and hold fast. A red squirrel, coming down the tree, stopped in great surprise when it saw her, and then ran away along a branch. Bravely, she climbed upward.

Light was just appearing in the eastern sky, and the small song-birds began to sing their welcome to the new day. Higher and higher Sylvia climbed. Her fingers ached from holding on, and the roughness of the branches hurt her feet. But on she went. Perhaps the old pine-tree welcomed this stranger among its branches, and loved the brave, beating heart of the gray-eyed child.

At last, Sylvia's face appeared like a pale star, and she stood, tired and aching, but bright with victory, high in the tree-top. Yes, there was the sea in the east, with the sun making a golden path across it. And in the west, the woods and farms, the green fields and white villages, reached miles into the distance. Truly, it was a great and beautiful world.

The birds sang louder and louder, and the sun grew brighter. Sylvia could see the white sails of ships out at sea, and the purple-pink clouds began to turn white. Where was the white heron's nest in this sea of green branches?

Now look down, Sylvy, to where the green marsh lies between the trees. There, where you saw the white heron once, you will see him again. Look, look! Something white is flying upward from the dead hemlock-tree by the green marsh. It comes higher and higher, and flies past the great

*It comes higher and higher, and flies past the great pine-tree,
its white wings beating slowly.*

pine-tree, its white wings beating slowly. Now it lands on a branch nearby, and cries back to his mate on the nest below and cleans his feathers for the new day.

The child watches, her heart full of happiness. She knows the wild white heron's secret now. In a minute he flies away, back down to his home in the green world below.

Then Sylvia begins the dangerous climb down, careful not to look down, and ready to cry sometimes because her fingers ache and her feet hurt. But she wonders over and over again what the young man will say to her when she tells him how to find his way straight to the heron's nest.

'Sylvy, Sylvy!' called the busy old grandmother again and again, but Sylvia's small bed was empty.

The visitor woke up, and hurried to get ready for his day in the woods. He was sure from the shy little girl's face that she knew where the white heron was.

Here she is now, paler than ever, her dress dirty from the pine-tree. The grandmother and the hunter stand at the door together and question her, and the great moment has come to speak of the dead hemlock-tree by the green marsh.

But Sylvia does not speak after all, although the young man's kind eyes are looking straight into her own. He can make them rich with money; he has promised it, and they are poor now. She wants so much to make him happy, and he waits to hear the story that she can tell.

No, she must keep silent! Why, suddenly, is it forbidden to speak? It is the first time in her young life that the great world has put out a hand to her – and must she push it away, because of a bird?

The sound of the great pine-tree's branches is in her ears, she remembers how the white heron came flying through the golden air and how they watched the sea and the morning together, and Sylvia cannot speak; she cannot tell the heron's secret and give its life away.

The pain in that loyal heart was great when the young man went away disappointed later in the day. The promise and the dream of love had gone for ever. For a long time she heard again his whistle as she came home with the cow, and she even forgot her sadness at the sound of his gun and the song-birds falling silent to the ground. Were the birds better friends than their hunter – who can tell? But remember, you wild creatures of the woodland, what this child has lost! Bring your love and trust and tell your secrets to this lonely country child!

By Courier

O. Henry

At this time of year, and this time of day, there were very few people in the park. It was probable that the young lady, who was sitting on one of the benches, had just wanted to rest for a while and think about the coming spring.

She sat there, thoughtful and still. The sadness in her eyes seemed to be something new, because it had not yet changed her bright young face, nor turned her soft lips into a thin hard line.

A tall young man came walking through the park along the path near the bench where she was sitting. Behind him came a boy carrying a suitcase. When the man saw the young lady, his face changed to red and back to pale again. He watched her face as he came closer, and his own face showed both hope and worry at the same time.

He passed her only a few meters away, but she gave no sign that she had seen him, or even knew he was there.

Fifty meters further on the young man suddenly stopped and sat down on a bench by the path. The boy dropped the suitcase and stared at him with wondering eyes. The young man took out his handkerchief and wiped his face. It was a good handkerchief, a good face, and the young man was good to look at. He said to the boy:

'I want you to take a message to that young lady on that bench. Tell her I am on my way to the station, to leave for San Francisco. From there I shall travel north to the wild places of Alaska. Tell her that, as she has ordered me neither to speak nor to write to her, I am taking this chance to appeal to her one last time. Tell her that she has been unkind and unjust to someone who has done no wrong; and she has given him no reasons and no explanations. Tell her that I do not believe her to be an unjust person. Tell her that I have disobeyed her orders, in the hope that she will return to the paths of justice and reason. Go, and tell her that.'

The young man dropped a half-dollar into the boy's hand. The boy looked at him for a moment with bright, intelligent eyes out of a dirty face, then turned and ran down the path. As he came closer to the lady on the bench, he studied her carefully. The lady looked back at him coolly.

'Lady,' the boy said, 'that guy on the other bench sent yer a song and dance by me. If yer don't know the guy, and he's tryin' to do some funny business, say the word, and I'll call a cop in three minutes. If yer does know him, and he's all right, then I'll give yer the song and dance that he gave me.'

The young lady showed a little, just a little interest.

'A song and dance!' she said, in a very sweet voice that seemed to suggest something not at all sweet. 'A new idea – a kind of traveling singer, I suppose. I used to know the gentleman who sent you, so it will not be necessary to call the police. Please begin your song and dance, but do not sing too loudly. It is not really the time or the place for that kind of thing.'

'Aw, come on, lady,' said the boy, 'yer know what I mean. It ain't a song and dance really, it's a lot of hot air. He told me to tell you he's got his shirts in that case and he's movin' on to 'Frisco. Then he's goin' on up to Alaska. He says yer told him not to send round no more love notes, nor stand around lookin' over the garden gate. He says yer threw him out like last year's hat, and never gave him no chance to argue. He says yer told him to go, and never said why.'

'*He says yer threw him out like last year's hat,*' *said the boy.*

The interest in the young lady's eyes did not go away. Perhaps her interest was in the cleverness of the future Alaskan traveler, who had found a way to get round her orders. She fixed her eyes on an untidy-looking tree in the park, and spoke to the messenger:

'Tell the gentleman that he knows very well what my ideals are. He knows what they have been, and he knows what they still are. In this matter, the two most important ideals are that a person should be true, and loyal. Tell him that I have studied my own heart, and I know that it can be weak, as well as strong. That is why I do not wish to listen to his arguments or to hear any words from him at all. I am not unjust, and have never been unjust. But if he really wants to hear what he already knows, you may tell him this . . .

'Tell him I entered the garden room that evening from the door at the back, to cut a flower for my mother. Tell him I saw him and Miss Ashburton beneath the pink oleander bush. It was a pretty picture indeed, but the juxtaposition told the whole story without the need for a single word. I left the garden room at once, without the flower, and with my ideals broken into a hundred thousand pieces. You may take that song and dance to your dancing teacher.'

'Juxta . . . juxta? Help me out, lady,' said the boy. 'Give me an easier word, will yer?'

'Juxtaposition . . . or, if you like, closeness – the kind of closeness that can destroy an ideal in a second.'

At once the boy turned and ran back to the other bench. The young man's eyes questioned him, hungrily. The boy's eyes shone with excitement at his new job as translator.

'The lady says that she knows that girls just can't stop listenin' when a guy comes tellin' stories and tryin' to be real nice and friendly. That's why she won't listen to no sweet words from yer. She says she caught yer in the hothouse under the flowers with yer arms around a girl. She just stepped in the back to get a flower for her ma, and yer was holdin' this other girl real nice and close. She says it looked pretty, all right all right, but the juxta . . . but it made her sick. She says yer gotta get busy and get off and get that train real quick.'

The young man's eyes opened wide and his eyes lit up with a sudden thought. His hand flew to the inside pocket of his coat, and pulled out a handful of letters. Choosing one, he gave it to the boy, together with a silver dollar from another pocket.

'Give that letter to the lady,' he said, 'and ask her to read it. Tell her that it should explain everything. Tell her that she needs another ideal – she must learn to trust, and that trust can prevent much unnecessary heartache. Tell her that her ideals are not broken. Tell her that the true and loyal person is still true and loyal, and has not changed in any way. Tell her I am waiting for an answer.'

The messenger stood before the lady again.

'The guy says there's been bad things said about him, and it ain't right, it ain't just. He says he ain't a bad guy. And, lady, yer read that letter, and you're goin' to see that he's all right, all right.'

The young lady took the letter. She seemed unsure about it, but she opened it, and read it.

Dear Dr Arnold

I want to thank you for the very kind help that you gave to my daughter last Friday evening, when she became suddenly ill with her old heart trouble in the garden room at Mrs Waldron's party. It was so lucky that you were near enough to catch her as she fell, and were able to give her a doctor's care at once. We are sure that you saved her life. I would be happy if you would visit us soon as her doctor.

Gratefully yours,

Robert Ashburton

The young lady closed the letter, and gave it back to the boy.

'The guy wants an answer,' said the messenger. 'What's the word, lady?'

The lady's eyes were suddenly very bright and smiling.

'Tell that guy on the other bench,' she said, with a happy, shaky little laugh, 'that his girl wants him.'

GLOSSARY

appeal to ask in a serious way for something important
approve to think that something is good or suitable
bench a long seat for two or more people, e.g. in a park
bow (*v*) to bend your head forward to show respect
bride a woman on the day of her wedding, and just afterwards
bush a plant like a small tree with lots of branches
cage a 'box' of metal bars in which birds or animals are kept
cop (*informal*) a police officer
creature any living thing that is not a plant
deaf-mute not able to hear or speak
deceive to make somebody believe something that is not true
disapprove to think that something is bad or not suitable
drunk having drunk too much alcohol and often behaving badly
embarrassed feeling shy or worried about what other people
  think of you
embarrassing something that makes you feel embarrassed
engaged if two people are engaged, they have agreed to marry
feather one of the light soft things that cover a bird's body
feeling (*n*) something that you feel inside yourself
flush when your face goes red because you are embarrassed
fool (*adj* **foolish**) a person who does something silly or stupid
forbidden when something is not allowed
forgive to stop being angry with someone for a bad thing that
  they did
fury (*adj* **furious**) very strong anger
gentleman a polite word for a man
guy (*informal*) a man
handkerchief a small piece of cloth used for blowing your nose

hunt to chase wild animals or birds to shoot or kill them

hunter a person who hunts wild animals

ideal (*n*) an idea or way of behaving that you think is perfect

just fair and right; unjust not fair or right

juxtaposition putting people or things close together

landlady a woman who rents a house to people for money

loyal staying true and faithful to somebody or something

maid a female servant

marsh soft wet ground

marshal (**in the US**) a kind of police officer

mate one of a male/female pair of birds or animals

mesquite a North American tree

nervous afraid and worried

nest a place where a bird keeps its eggs

pale with not much colour in the face

permit to allow

porter a person whose job is to carry people's luggage

Pullman (**coach**) a very comfortable coach on a train

puzzled not understanding

revolver a handgun

rifle a gun with a long barrel which you hold to your shoulder

saloon a bar where alcoholic drinks were sold in the US in the past

sand a powdery earth that is found on beaches and in deserts

shy not able to talk easily to people you do not know

sneak to move towards somebody very quietly

spyglass (*NAmE*) a small telescope

stuffed when a dead animal or bird is filled with material, to keep its shape and appearance

thoughtful thinking a lot

trust to believe that somebody is honest and good

victory   success in a fight or a game or a great effort of some kind
whistle (*n*)   the long high sound made by blowing air between
   your lips
wooing (*old-fashioned*)   when a man tries to persuade a woman
   to love him and marry him
yell   to shout loudly

Non-standard forms used in the story

ain't   am not / isn't / aren't
an'   and
goin' / tellin', etc.   going / telling, etc.
gotta   got to
o'   of
s'pose   suppose
yer   you

ACTIVITIES

Before Reading

1 **Read the back cover of the book, and the introduction on the first page. What can you guess now about these stories? Choose one answer to each question.**

1 *The Kiss.* What does the kiss in this story do?
   a) It leads to a marriage.   c) It embarrasses someone.
   b) It ends a friendship.

2 *The Bride Comes to Yellow Sky.* Who does the Texan gunman want to fight in this story?
   a) Jack's new wife.   c) The wife's mother.
   b) Jack.

3 *A Seashore Wooing.* What do the girl and the boy in this story do about the Aunt Martha problem?
   a) They meet secretly.   c) They run away together.
   b) They just talk on the phone.

4 *The White Heron.* What do you think happens to the heron in this story?
   a) Somebody shoots it.   c) It dies naturally.
   b) The little girl saves it.

5 *By Courier.* What do you think the young man in this story has done wrong?
   a) Nothing.   c) Kissed another woman.
   b) Forgotten to send his girl some flowers.

ACTIVITIES

After Reading

1 **Here are the thoughts of five characters (one from each story). Which characters are they, and from which story? Who or what are they thinking about?**

1 'Here she is again, and yes! She's looking this way through her spyglass. What a sweet pretty face she has! And I'm sure she's Connie's friend. And if she is, she'll know the deaf-mute alphabet, because Connie taught it to her . . .'

2 'Am I going to find it today? Is my luck going to change? I was watching her face last night, and she knows where it is – I'm sure of it. But she's so shy; she's almost too afraid to speak. But they need the money, that's clear . . .'

3 'Is he still there on the bench? No, I mustn't look at him, I absolutely mustn't look! The boy's coming back! What's he going to say this time? Quick, I must look bored. I'm not in the least bit interested in *any* message from him . . .'

4 'They're not going to like it. They'll never forgive me for not telling them first. And it's too late to send a message now – the train will be there in an hour. We'll just have to get home as quick as we can and hope no one sees us . . .'

5 'I knew it was too good to be true. How could she possibly care for me? She was just being kind, I suppose. It's very clear that he's more than a friend. Perhaps they're engaged already. He's good-looking, a friend of the family . . .'

2 In *The Kiss,* how did Mr Harvy feel when he heard Nathalie
   was going to marry Mr Brantain? He is talking to Nathalie's
   brother here. Use these words to complete what he says.

   believe / dull / embarrassed / kissed / know / liked / love /
   loved / marry / money / punish / reason / rich

   'I don't _____ it! How can she possibly _____ that _____
   little man? I thought she _____ me – in fact, I thought she
   _____ me! Yes, I know she was _____ when I _____ her in
   front of Brantain, but I didn't _____ he was in the room. Ah!
   Just a minute . . . Brantain is very _____, isn't he? So that's
   the _____! She wants _____, not _____. Well, I must find a
   way to _____ her for the way she has behaved to me.'

3 *A Seashore Wooing* ends with a question: What *will* Aunt
   Martha say? Write a paragraph to give a new ending to the
   story. Choose one of these ideas, or think of your own idea.

   1 Very angry / refuses to speak to Marguerite / sends
      Marguerite away / Marguerite stays with Mrs Allardyce until
      wedding / Mrs Saxby explains / man broke Aunt Martha's
      heart when young / letter comes / no money for Marguerite
      after death / Marguerite marries Francis

   2 Angry at first / you deceived me / making terrible mistake /
      Mrs Shelmardine visits / Aunt Martha says Marguerite still
      too young / must wait a year / takes Marguerite travelling in
      Europe / Marguerite meets a handsome Italian / falls in love
      again / Aunt Martha angry again

   3 Meets Francis / likes him / agrees to wedding next month

4 Here are two conversations: one between Jack Potter and his wife at the end of *The Bride Comes to Yellow Sky*, and the other between Sylvia and her grandmother at the end of *A White Heron*. Match each question with an answer, then put them into two separate conversations.

QUESTIONS

1 'Did you know where that white heron's nest was, Sylvia?'

2 'Who was that, Jack? Oh, I was so frightened! I thought he was going to kill you!'

3 'Why did he want to fight you?'

4 'So why didn't you tell that nice young man where it was?'

5 'He ain't coming back, is he, Jack? I know I won't sleep at night if that man's outside the house.'

6 'But what about the money, Sylvia? Did you forget that? We needed those ten dollars!'

ANSWERS

7 'It's not personal. He always goes out lookin' for a fight with someone when he's drunk.'

8 'I don't know. It didn't seem right; it wasn't my secret. And I didn't want that beautiful bird to die.'

9 'That was Scratchy Wilson. He's crazy when he's drunk – but he's all right when he's not drunk.'

10 'Yes, I know. I was thinking about it all night – all the things that we could buy . . .'

11 'No, he ain't coming back. You saw how he was. He knows I'm married now.'

12 'Yes, I found out this morning. I climbed up a very tall pine-tree and saw the heron flying to its nest.'

5 Here are some different titles for the five stories. Decide which title fits each story best. Which title would you choose for each story – one of these, or the original title? Why?

- Sylvia's Choice
- Love Through a Spyglass
- Gold-digger
- Scratchy's Surprise
- Forbidden Meeting
- The Park Bench Argument
- A Bad Day to Come Home
- The Heron Hunter
- The Messenger
- A Heart Full of Money

6 There are, or will be, four marriages in these love stories. Do you think they will all be successful marriages? Can you see any problems for these people? Write a few sentences to give your opinions. Use the questions below to help you.

1 Nathalie and Mr Brantain. Are their reasons for marrying the same? Will this be a problem, do you think?

2 Jack Potter and Mrs Potter. Will the new Mrs Potter be happy in Yellow Sky? How will Jack's friends and the people of Yellow Sky behave towards her?

3 Marguerite Forrester and Francis Shelmardine. How old do you think Marguerite is? Is it a good idea to marry the first boy that you meet and fall in love with?

4 The young lady and the young man in the park. (Let's call them Jane and Dick.) Are they going to have a lot of arguments and misunderstandings, do you think? If they do, does it matter?

7 Which story in this book did you like best, and which did you like least? Explain why you think this.

ABOUT THE AUTHORS

KATE CHOPIN

Kate Chopin (1850–1904) was born Catherine O'Flaherty to an Irish–French family in St Louis, Missouri, in the USA. She was brought up speaking French and English, and was a great reader. In 1870 she married Oscar Chopin, but he died in 1882, leaving her with six young children. She wrote poetry and short stories for journals, and later, published two collections, *Bayou Folk* (1894) and *A Night in Acadie* (1897). In her time she was famous for her adventurous writing, which explored women's lives and feelings in new and sometimes shocking ways.

STEPHEN CRANE

Stephen Crane (1871–1900) was born in New Jersey, USA, the fourteenth child of a church minister. He was a novelist, short-story writer, poet, and journalist, and also traveled in Cuba and Greece as a war reporter. For a time he lived in England, where he became friendly with writers such as Joseph Conrad. His most famous work, *The Red Badge of Courage* (1895), a novel about the American Civil War, was a great success in both America and England. During his short life, Crane achieved great fame for his sensitive, realistic stories, which have made him a classic figure in American literature.

LUCY MAUD MONTGOMERY

Lucy Maud Montgomery (1874–1942) was born on Prince Edward Island, in Canada. Her mother died when she was two years old, and she went to live with her grandparents on their farm. For a while she was a teacher, but after her grandfather's death, she returned to the farm to take care of her grandmother. By now she was already earning money from her short story writing. In 1908 her first book, *Anne of Green Gables*, was published, and was an immediate success. She went on to write several more books about Anne, who became one of the most internationally popular characters in children's literature.

SARAH ORNE JEWETT

Sarah Orne Jewett (1849–1909) was born in Maine, USA. She was often taken by her doctor father on his visits to the fishermen and farmers of Maine, and she came to love their vanishing way of life, and the sights and sounds of the Maine countryside. She wrote poetry, novels, and short stories, and her first important story was published in *Atlantic Monthly* at the age of nineteen. Her writing gave detailed and sympathetic pictures of the lives of local people. Her most famous work is *The Country of the Pointed Firs* (1896), a short novel which describes the changes that come to a Maine seaport town.

O. HENRY

O. Henry (1862–1910) was born William Sydney Porter in North Carolina, USA. When he was twenty, he went to work in a bank in Texas, and soon began to write short stories. In 1898 he was accused of stealing money from a bank, and was sent to prison for three years. He continued to write stories in prison, and when he left in 1901, he was a successful and famous writer. During his life he wrote about 600 stories; some of the best-known ones are *The Gift of the Magi, The Ransom of Red Chief*, and *The Cop and the Anthem*.

OXFORD BOOKWORMS LIBRARY

Classics • Crime & Mystery • Factfiles • Fantasy & Horror
Human Interest • Playscripts • Thriller & Adventure
True Stories • World Stories

The OXFORD BOOKWORMS LIBRARY provides enjoyable reading in English, with a wide range of classic and modern fiction, non-fiction, and plays. It includes original and adapted texts in seven carefully graded language stages, which take learners from beginner to advanced level. An overview is given on the next pages.

All Stage 1 titles are available as audio recordings, as well as over eighty other titles from Starter to Stage 6. All Starters and many titles at Stages 1 to 4 are specially recommended for younger learners. Every Bookworm is illustrated, and Starters and Factfiles have full-colour illustrations.

The OXFORD BOOKWORMS LIBRARY also offers extensive support. Each book contains an introduction to the story, notes about the author, a glossary, and activities. Additional resources include tests and worksheets, and answers for these and for the activities in the books. There is advice on running a class library, using audio recordings, and the many ways of using Oxford Bookworms in reading programmes. Resource materials are available on the website <www.oup.com/bookworms>.

The *Oxford Bookworms Collection* is a series for advanced learners. It consists of volumes of short stories by well-known authors, both classic and modern. Texts are not abridged or adapted in any way, but carefully selected to be accessible to the advanced student.

You can find details and a full list of titles in the *Oxford Bookworms Library Catalogue* and *Oxford English Language Teaching Catalogues*, and on the website <www.oup.com/bookworms>.

THE OXFORD BOOKWORMS LIBRARY
GRADING AND SAMPLE EXTRACTS

STARTER • 250 HEADWORDS

present simple – present continuous – imperative –
can/cannot, must – going to (future) – simple gerunds ...

Her phone is ringing – but where is it?
Sally gets out of bed and looks in her bag. No phone.
She looks under the bed. No phone. Then she looks
behind the door. There is her phone. Sally picks up her
phone and answers it. *Sally's Phone*

STAGE 1 • 400 HEADWORDS

... past simple – coordination with *and, but, or* –
subordination with *before, after, when, because, so* ...

I knew him in Persia. He was a famous builder and I
worked with him there. For a time I was his friend, but
not for long. When he came to Paris, I came after him –
I wanted to watch him. He was a very clever, very
dangerous man. *The Phantom of the Opera*

STAGE 2 • 700 HEADWORDS

... present perfect – *will* (future) – *(don't) have to, must not, could* –
comparison of adjectives – simple *if* clauses – past continuous –
tag questions – *ask/tell* + infinitive ...

While I was writing these words in my diary, I decided
what to do. I must try to escape. I shall try to get down
the wall outside. The window is high above the ground,
but I have to try. I shall take some of the gold with me – if
I escape, perhaps it will be helpful later. *Dracula*

STAGE 3 • 1000 HEADWORDS
... should, may – present perfect continuous – *used to* – past perfect –
causative – relative clauses – indirect statements ...

Of course, it was most important that no one should see
Colin, Mary, or Dickon entering the secret garden. So Colin
gave orders to the gardeners that they must all keep away
from that part of the garden in future. *The Secret Garden*

STAGE 4 • 1400 HEADWORDS
... past perfect continuous – passive (simple forms) –
would conditional clauses – indirect questions –
relatives with *where/when* – gerunds after prepositions/phrases ...

I was glad. Now Hyde could not show his face to the world
again. If he did, every honest man in London would be
proud to report him to the police. *Dr Jekyll and Mr Hyde*

STAGE 5 • 1800 HEADWORDS
... future continuous – future perfect –
passive (modals, continuous forms) –
would have conditional clauses – modals + perfect infinitive ...

If he had spoken Estella's name, I would have hit him. I was
so angry with him, and so depressed about my future, that I
could not eat the breakfast. Instead I went straight to the old
house. *Great Expectations*

STAGE 6 • 2500 HEADWORDS
... passive (infinitives, gerunds) – advanced modal meanings –
clauses of concession, condition

When I stepped up to the piano, I was confident. It was as if
I knew that the prodigy side of me really did exist. And when I
started to play, I was so caught up in how lovely I looked that I
didn't worry how I would sound. *The Joy Luck Club*

BOOKWORMS · HUMAN INTEREST · STAGE 3

Love Story

ERICH SEGAL

Retold by Rosemary Border

This is a love story you won't forget. Oliver Barrett meets Jenny Cavilleri. He plays sports, she plays music. He's rich, and she's poor. They argue, and they fight, and they fall in love.

So they get married, and make a home together. They work hard, they enjoy life, they make plans for the future. Then they learn that they don't have much time left.

Their story has made people laugh, and cry, all over the world.

BOOKWORMS · WORLD STORIES · STAGE 3

A Cup of Kindness: Stories from Scotland

Retold by Jennifer Bassett

In Edinburgh a detective listens to a confession; in Orkney an old man lives with the ghosts of his past. In the Outer Hebrides some travellers learn a lesson; in Glasgow a young woman steals a meeting with a famous actor; and in a small town somewhere a pigeon dies. These stories are as richly varied as the land of Scotland itself.

Bookworms World Stories collect stories written in English from around the world. This volume has stories by Scottish writers Eona Macnicol, Malcolm Laing, Ian Rankin, George Mackay Brown, and Susie Maguire.